SCRIBBLED POETRY

THE FINEST COLLECTION.

ANIL A.

Contents

Foreword

Writing is something that flows naturally. It's the Lord's gift to someone who can think and exhibit those beautiful thoughts on a piece of paper. The poets whose work I have compiled in this book can be seen to show their immense energy, and command over their thoughts and words.

This book is one that will always remain close to me; the poems in this holding real value.

Acknowledgements

My deepest acknowledgement to the editor Dr. Rai and the various authors whose works I have compliled to create this book of scribbled poetry.

1. Just the end

It wrecks me, that last moment
that played out so wrong.
Our hopeless eyes locked
just a few seconds too long.

And my eyes begged yours
to ask me to stay.
And your eyes welled up
as you walked away.
Amy O'Connor

2. Don't walk away

I watch you walk away from me,
And the tears start to fall.
I ask myself a million times,
How did we lose it all?
For the first time I had no words
That to you I could say.
I cling to old memories
And I watch you walk away.
I just don't want to let you go,
But inside I know I must.
My heart's whimpering with pain,
But it's my mind I trust.
There's confusion around me,
There's numbness in my heart,
But looking at you walk away
My world just fell apart.
If only I could handle it
And bear to just say,
I'd use my breath and say the words:
Don't Walk Away!
-Sara Jain

3. Last forever

You are my best friend; you belong in my heart.

We go through ups and downs, but still nothing can tear us apart.

I know you as a sister, and I will always care.

Love, respect, and trust are the things we share.

I know you as a person; I especially know you as a friend.

Our friendship is something that will never end.

Right now, this second, this minute, this day,

Our sisterhood is here, is here to stay.

My friendship with you is special and true.

When we are together, we stick like glue.

When I'm in the darkness that needs some light,

When you're by my side, I know things are all right.

Our friendship is so strong; it breaks down bars.

Our friendship is also bright, like the sun and the stars.

If we were in a competition for friendships, we would get a gold,

Because responsibility and cleverness are the keys we hold.

I met you as a stranger, took you as a friend.

I hope our long friendship will never end.

Our friendship is like a magnet; it pulls us together,

Because no matter where we are, our friendship will last forever!

-Mia Jaswal

4. The last letter

I'm still hanging on to the memories we made
Still fresh as the summer and untarnished as a jade
Do you still remember the love that we shared?
That evening, in the patio, into each other's eyes when we stared
That moment when all the clocks went still
And time seemed like a paralysed soul
That glance of yours, your glittering eyes
Our very first chance and our very first stroll
I prayed to God, "May time have mercy and let me treasure her presence tonight"
You looked like the immensity of the sky and I was a meagre meandering kite
You smelled of the spring, the florets of lavender, your cheeks as rubescent as the petals of rose
I held your hand and your heart set aflame like a blaze of fire amidst the first fall of snow
The night went on and we stayed awake just to vow to grow old together
The heat of the moment, the nightly hue, we knew that it was now or never
With the same promises in our hearts and souls, the night ended, but holding hands, there we stood
I pledged my life that we'd never part but the very thing happened, that I wished, never would

With the gentleness of the air and the calm of a storm, you left my hand and swayed away
To a universe where I had never been, the place where you'd forever stay
You took the light away that day
The only light that kept me alive
I longed for the day you'd come back and hold my hand again
But I knew that day would never arrive
The sun doesn't shine as bright as then and the daffodils don't dance anymore
Neither do the leaves look as green, nor do the lemons taste that sour
You snatched the seasons away forever and with that you snatched my will to live
I won't stay here anymore and neither will you, but our memories always will
I'll meet you there in your universe soon, when the time will again stand still.
I'll meet you there in your universe soon, when the time will again stand still.
-Jahnavi Kulkarni

5. Range

Stretch above land, into their peak,
It is the sky, they constantly seek.
In the far distance, we notice their height,
A view from the top - spectacular site!
Closely positioned, to form a range,
Human eyes, won't notice them change.
Not a prisoner, to immediate time,
Challenges many; unforgiving climb.
So much more, beyond their beauty,
Sheltering species, that is their duty,
Mountains are members, of the nature we know,
Way at the top, they often have snow.
-Tres Carl

6. Anatomy of a heartbreak

• 7 •

Eyes.

Heartbreak is her sunlit memory barely held by a wooden clothespin. It hangs and glares before your eyes, mocking as it fades into an empty filmstrip. Heartbreak is a lost soul left to perish in her ghost-town, and warmer sunsets are lifetimes away. A wonderwall left standing, pinned polaroids, desperate scratches. You had fought hard and long, for this, but homes are made for breaking and crumbling and leaving, especially in the losing side.

Mouth.

Heartbreak is a paper-tag of a goodbye caught in her lips. It is a metaphor that melts at the soft space under your tongue, a certain bittersweet taste made for drowning with a cold lager, a stranger's whispers, and the perils of his unfiltered cigarette kiss. Heartbreak is taming a manic scream into a delicate, defeated sigh, out of sync with the way she breathed. But then sighing still hurts, and breathing still hurts because you're alive.

Fray Narte

7. I tried

I tried so hard.
I tried my best.
I gave you my all,
And now there's nothing left.
You stole my heart
Then tore it in two.
Now I'm falling apart
And don't know what to do.
Divided by decisions,
Burned by the fire,
Confused by your words,
Tempted by desire.
I'm living in the present.
My mind is on the past.
Not knowing what I'll lose,
Not knowing what will last.
Blinded by fear,
Drowning in doubt,
Struggling to be free,
Looking for a way out.
-Sharvari Shah

8. It was

At night I lie

Thinking about all the things that died

When we parted ways

Could it be the perfect dayTo let you know

That I miss you, although

Things will never work out between us.

Even after you left me

I still found myself craving your hugs for free

Because our lives have been entangled completely

Without the hope of getting back together

I wish we could last forever

My heart aches, and my chest breaks

Knowing we lost something great

And even though we are not mates

I hope we could one day relate And finally, turn out to be friends

I know I made the worst mistake

And with a heavy heart, I earnestly pray

That you find it in your heart to forgive my ways

Lest I end up miserable till the end of my days.

Thinking about what we would be

Sparks a sad reality within me

That turns into a flame

Eventually leaving me weary and afraid

Come back to me. Let us do things differently

I promise to love you reverently

And keep you by my side comfortably

Walking down the streets every day,

I experience a sense of nostalgia

Realizing we were living on borrowed time

So many memories, so many investments together But still, lies managed to pull

us from each other

I am sorry. Now and forever.

Warm tears falling down my cheek

My heart pounding like a stray dog in a cage

My life trickling down as I grow in age

And struggling not to fall out in rage

I hope that this heavy wage

Will bring forth a blessing that has no break.

Am I going crazy?

Is this truly over between us, baby?

Weren't we supposed to grow old and forever be lazy?

I am still in shock and stress

For the love we shared was too strong to profess

But time would finally make this a mess.

Klaire B

9. Blighted Love

Flowers are fresh, and bushes green,
Cheerily the linnets sing;
Winds are soft, and skies serene;
Time, however, soon shall throw
Winter's snow
O'er the buxom breast of Spring!
Hope, that buds in lover's heart,
Lives not through the scorn of years;
Time makes love itself depart;
Time and scorn congeal the mind,—
Looks unkind
Freeze affection's warmest tears.
Time shall make the bushes green;
Time dissolve the winter snow;
Winds be soft, and skies serene;
Linnets sing their wonted strain:
But again
Blighted love shall never blow!
Kamna Patil

10. Bodily

The lancet of my inner eye
Has pierced the clot of clouds apart
To reveal in the depths of sky
The globule of my heart.

Pulsating in a cage of ribs
You break into a shower of pain;
Whirlpool, you suck into your lips
The viscin of my brain.

The cerebellum in my skull
Compressed by cacophony breaks
Into a lava-throated gull
And spitting fangs of snakes.

Scream silently and scream once more,
The tongue is ripped and torn;
Scream silently a savage O,
For what is dead is gone!
Tanmay Jain